FOR NIRVANA

For Nirvana *108 Zen Sijo Poems*

CHO OH-HYUN

introduction by **KWON YOUNGMIN**
translated by **HEINZ INSU FENKL**

Columbia University Press 〰 **NEW YORK**

COLUMBIA UNIVERSITY PRESS
Publishers Since 1893
NEW YORK   CHICHESTER, WEST SUSSEX

cup.columbia.edu
Translation copyright © 2016 Heinz Insu Fenkl

Library of Congress Cataloging-in-Publication Data
Names: Cho, O-hyŏn, 1932– author. | Fenkl, Heinz Insu, 1960– translator. | Kwŏn, Yŏng-min, 1948– author of introduction.
Title: For nirvana : 108 zen sijo poems / Cho O-hyŏn ; introduction by Kwŏn Yŏng-min ; translated by Heinz Insu Fenkl.
Other titles: Poems. English
Description: New York : Columbia University Press, 2016. | Includes bibliographical references.
Identifiers: LCCN 2016002181 (print) | LCCN 2016016304 (ebook) | ISBN 9780231179904 (cloth : alk. paper) | ISBN 9780231179911 (pbk. : alk. paper) | ISBN 9780231542432 (e-book) | ISBN 9780231542432 ()
Classification: LCC PL992.17.024 A2 2016 (print) | LCC PL992.17.024 (ebook) | DDC 895.71/4—dc23
LC record available at https://lccn.loc.gov/2016002181

BOOK & COVER DESIGN: CHANG JAE LEE
COVER IMAGE: JOSEF HOFLEMNER © GALLERY STOCK

☺

c   10 9 8 7 6 5 4 3 2 1
p   10 9 8 7 6 5 4 3 2 1

CONTENTS

ix

CONTENTS

—The moon in the water

IT WAS NIGHTTIME and everyone else was sleeping. Under the calm moonlight, the tree branches cast mottled patterns against the pale skin on the paper doors of the temple rooms. Mr. Kim—a lay Buddhist student who was pondering the question, "What is the self?"—couldn't get to sleep, and so he had come out into the courtyard. He walked for a while there, treading through the sound of wind chimes that seemed to carry no more than knee-high from the ground. That's when he saw the stranger sitting there, at the edge of Gwaneum Pond, with his arms hugging his knees to his chest. "In the middle of the night?" Kim thought. Even as his hair stood on end, something made him go and stand behind the young man and keep a watchful eye. Perhaps the man sensed Kim's presence, perhaps not—he just stared at the deep, mysterious reflection of the moon floating on the water. He sat there, not moving, like some hastily packed bundle of baggage. Just then, the moon shifted, drawing up its own shadowy reflection, and a misty drizzle began to come down. The stranger stood up on his feet as if he were a weak, old man. "Well, I'll be . . . ," he said. "You can look at the moon in the water but you can never scoop it out . . ." Kim watched him rub his hands over his haggard face and stagger out of the temple gates as dawn was breaking.

—Musan Cho Oh-hyun, March 2015

ON MUSAN CHO OH-HYUN'S SIJO

Kwon Youngmin, senior advisor, the Manhae Foundation

1

IT HAS BEEN ten years already since the inaugural Manhae Festival, when I first found my way to Baekdamsa Temple. I was to present a paper at the symposium there on the literary works of the great Buddhist poet Han Yongun. Baekdamsa is the place to which Han Yongun returned in 1922 after he was released from West Gate Prison in Seoul. He had been arrested as one of the masterminds of the 1919 March First independence movement and imprisoned there by the Japanese authorities for more than two years. Han Yongun, better known today by his Buddhist name, Manhae, wrote the poems for his collection *The Silence of Love* (1926) at Baekdamsa. Even now the creative origins of the poems in that book are veiled and obscure, but this small mountain temple deep in the valley has become a literary sanctuary that has given rise to one of the great mysteries of Korean literature.

On the grounds of Baekdamsa, as I was lost in thought about Manhae Han Yongun, I unexpectedly met a venerable senior monk who, in his humble robe, looked just like Manhae. As I entered with my group, he came up to me with his hands pressed together in greeting and asked me who I was. I returned his bow and told him I was a professor who taught literature at a university. I added that I was also a literary critic.

He laughed loudly upon hearing that. "So," he said, "You're one of those people with an attachment to a useless discipline. Literary criticism . . ."

I was shocked. I had just met this old monk for the first time and I had no idea how to respond to this kind of conversation, so I just laughed along with him.

"You write all those reviews, but it's all a useless enterprise. You're just trawling for writing that has a unique use of language. It's easy for your kind of writing to lack integrity."

I was dumbstruck. In my many decades of work as a literary critic, I had published books of just about every kind, and this old monk had just called it all a vain trawling enterprise.

He must have noticed the hardening expression on my face. He continued, "As for writing, your soul has to be in it for it to be authentic. But what passes for criticism these days is just taking a theory by one person and taking a work by someone else and arguing back and forth about who's right and who's wrong. That's why it's all in vain.

"There's an old story about a lake deep in a valley. One night a big fish swam up a waterfall and ascended into Heaven to become a dragon. People said there must be something left over from that event, so they cast their nets in water. But the fish had already ascended! What could they catch in their nets?" Finally, taking hold of my hand, the old monk said, "I'm just telling you this so we can laugh about it."

I took those words to heart. It seemed to me that he had pointed out the weak spot in my own study of literature. I was crestfallen.

Baekdamsa valley was roaring with the sound of water. I lifted my head and turned my attention to the high peaks of Seorak, which were shrouded in fog. The true character of Seorak was revealed to me then, and I had the sudden intense feeling that, for the first time in my life, I had encountered a wizard. I wondered about that old monk. Later, someone from the group quietly told me he was Musan Cho Oh-hyun, abbot of Shinheungsa Temple in the Mt. Seoraksan complex. Once again, I was shocked.

My first meeting with Master Cho was a gift of fate, and now I visit Baekdamsa Temple frequently. These days the road that enters Inner Seorak is maintained like an expressway, but Baekdam's valleys are still as remote as ever. There, the great old monk who looks like Manhae keeps vigil, and Manhae's spirit is still alive and overflowing throughout the valley.

Last year, after retiring from Seoul National University, where I had served for more than thirty years, I began the task of gathering together all the poems written by Musan Cho Oh-hyun, including his collections of sijo, and compiled and annotated *The Collected Works of Cho Oh-hyun* (from which this current volume is extracted). This was the only work I could show to Master Cho, who—ten years earlier, when I'd first met him—had made the cutting remark that to do literary criticism was like trawling in vain.

The task of assembling and organizing scattered materials, comparing variants, putting them in a chronology, and supplying the necessary annotations to provide an authoritative text for the next generation of readers—Master Cho was sure to be critical of this endeavor, to get angry at me again and say that it was all useless. But what was I to do? This was my role as a literary critic. Hadn't he already told me as much?

2

During the Joseon Dynasty, the great monks such as Hyujeong and Yujeong left many Zen poems, but they did not compose a single sijo. If one looks through Professor Jeong Byeong-uk's *The Dictionary of Literary Sijo*, among the hundreds of sijo poets during the Joseon Dynasty, there is not a single monk. Manhae wrote sijo after his enlightenment, but not a single sijo is included in *The Silence of Love*. In that context, the fact that Master Cho began his writing of poetry in the sijo form is not to be taken lightly. Master Cho embraced the sijo form fatefully and confronted it along with the numerous *hwadu*—the koan-like spiritual "head word" problems—of Korean Zen. His "Musan's Ten Bulls" depicts the realm of the ineffable, and his use of language in works like "Speechless Speech" and "Wordless Words" is a paradox. Like Zen *hwadu*, these works deconstruct language because Master Cho does not regard the poetic form of sijo as an innate ontological necessity.

In Master Cho's sijo, written under his Buddhist name, Musan, one initially discovers an emphasis on the beauty of restraint. To readers attuned to poetic sentiment, this sort of sijo teaches emotional restraint, which we can see is Musan's imperative for writing sijo. Indeed, where language is concerned, Musan is the great master who pioneered the genre of "Zen sijo" by elevating the language of sijo to parallel the *hwadu* of Zen.

While maintaining the three-part structure of sijo, which is one of its defining characteristics, Musan gives attention to its internal dynamism. The ultimate beauty of his sijo as a poetic form is that it aspires to an effect that only it can achieve. There are, however, many kinds of aesthetic self-regulation that are necessary for this form to be realized.

First, Musan's sijo are characterized by a regulation of speech. He eliminates unnecessary words for maximum economy, supplying in their place a minimal number of absolutely necessary words, thereby calming the reader's emotional exuberance and moderating the aesthetic impulse. The restrained diction in Musan's sijo is not meant to constrain language or to shackle it; it is restrained naturally within the structure, and the freedom that emerges within these constraints is integral to its unique beauty.

As Musan elevates the sijo form into the realm of Zen, he transcends the typical qualities of the convention, deconstructing it while creating a new poetic form. This new form, which interweaves different voices into one poetic expression, gives rise to a dynamic poetic tension and can be termed *iagijo*, or "story sijo." This new form of sijo goes beyond the aesthetic of symmetry and balance that sijo has traditionally featured; it establishes a broader and higher inclusive aesthetic.

Much as the spirit of sijo is to discover one human value within reality, Musan's story sijo includes the speech and sounds of all social classes. The voices rendered here in the conversational space are the voices of Buddhist monks in their temples, woodcutters deep in the mountains, and also common folk such as the street blacksmith. Because these voices reflect the condition of living speech, they are not expressed in a uniform vocabulary; the words are inherently in a dialogue, and as the dialogic quality inherent to these distinct voices emerges, it continually shapes the poetic moment.

For example, in "Speaking Without Speaking 1," Musan opens up a dynamic dialogic space poised in the formal structure of the sijo. Unlike a conventional sijo, which is characterized by an overarching point of view, "Speaking Without Speaking 1" includes diverse voices as part of that internal dialogic space. The poetic moment is transformed from static to dynamic, and this dynamism is made integral by the commonplace language used in the poem. The language in this work is not simply a matter of clashing diction—the collision and conflict of those levels of diction work like a catalyst. Musan gives that discursive action a concrete form by incorporating words from one vocabulary into a discourse with those from another; the diction of common speech constantly engages the other, higher, level of diction, catalyzing questions and answers.

"The Seagulls & the East Sea," which depicts an internal dialogue, represents a new kind of narrative poem—a form of sijo whose poetic space plays on the reader's presumption of narrative. The layered voices—which are immediate, realistic, and straightforward—interweave to create a unique kind of narrative that advances the text's the poetic sensibility. It is not an objective story that exists in objective reality, and it is not mediated by the poet's voice, yet it does not neglect the inflection that permeates the inner consciousness. And so, even while being the most prosaic of stories, it evokes a poetic mood—and by evoking a mood associated with the aesthetic of poetry, the poem becomes a new form: the "story sijo."

One could say that the extreme directness of Musan's sijo is due to the influence of Zen. Human speech and the sounds of nature are precisely the marks that indicate that reality is alive. The absence of sound signifies death. A human life gives rise to speech, and nature gives rise to sounds that signify its vitality; thus the perpetuation of life is human speech comingling with the sounds of nature into a single story. Musan composes sijo containing this speech and these sounds, these very living things, while as a poet he embarks on the path of a "Distant Holy Man."

Today, this one day,
　　on this one day called today

I saw the whole of the sun rise
　　and saw it all set

Nothing more to see—
　　a swarm of gnats laying eggs, dying

I am still alive,
　　long past my time to die,

But consider—today, I don't feel
　　as if I've lived even this single day

He may live a thousand years,
　　but the holy man

Is but a distant cloud of gnats

　　Language and sound cannot escape the constraints of time. But the poet, using the sounds of human speech and embracing the sounds of nature, *can* escape the bounds of time. What possibilities are there beyond the themes of beginnings and endings evoked by the words "the whole of the sun rise" and "saw it all set"? Musan, having already created a story sijo that reflects the sounds and voices of humanity, makes this question moot because, ultimately, it is in the place beyond existence that words become what we know as poetry....

FOR NIRVANA

BITTER FLOWER

in my younger days, my name
was wild apricot tree in a fertile field

bees and butterflies, the jealous spring—
i did not know about flowers then;

but on the day that Suni
went over the wall,
i knew that blood was red

DAYDREAM

White bellflower in the mountain,
    dandelion in the meadow;
the faint memory of my birthplace
    —a pensive face in the well.
Just once, I want to see her again—Suni,
    who stood with her back to the outfield wall.

I do not know if the light scent of wormwood
    has yet begun to rise
over that hill, where 10 *li* is such a long way;
    under the moon, too bright,
a small village secretively appears
    as I tread upon this indelible image.

This night—drink it and it does not fill,
    but memory's glass cannot be emptied.
It is a storage jar with a burning in the belly,
    somewhere, a spreading anxiety;
only echoes hang over the place
    where one awakens from sleep.

My life in this world—I've lived it badly to the last.
    But with the first water drawn from the well at dawn,
a single candle stick, and a bowl of rice,
    my mother's mother prayed over
this prince who was not allowed to play
    beside the stone statue that day.

DISTANT HOLY MAN

Today, this one day,
    on this one day called today

I saw the whole of the sun rise
    and saw it all set

Nothing more to see—
    a swarm of gnats laying eggs, dying

I am still alive,
    long past my time to die,

But consider—today, I don't feel
    as if I've lived even this single day

He may live a thousand years,
    but the holy man

Is but a distant cloud of gnats

3

FOR NIRVANA

ELM TREE & MOON

she a dragonfly's wings,
a filmy, rustling silk skirt,
and I a peacock shaft,
a mole upon her body

rise high, shine far
rise high, shine far

DESIRE, DEEPER THAN THE MARROW

You can't throw away an entire lifetime
Even for the sake of a god

Not rising, not sinking,
The mountain peony, just being,

Desire, deeper than the marrow,
Simply enfolded in its leaves

WHAT I'VE ALWAYS SAID

Love is the hand of a creeping vine,
green leaves that suck up
the taint of pollution, the taint of death,
the bright-red liquid metal
rust-water
that flows beneath
a steel-frame rebar concrete wall;
it embraces the whole world all at once.
It's a clutching clot of leaves.
Love is not talk—
it is the root of life.
You cannot name it, cannot draw the shape
of its heart and mind.
It is a clutching clot of leaves,
the dirty seed-leaf of the wild rose,
the bud-leaf of an oriental oak.

THE SOUND OF ANCIENT WOOD

One hears the sound of ancient wood
In the heart of an old tree

Only when the core is surely rotten
When all the straight limbs have snapped

And, naturally, some woody toxin
Remains in the crooked stump

THE DANCE & THE PATTERN

Late fall afternoon,
when death
crack-crackles underfoot,

sitting in a half-tub
of creek water,
I feel my forehead—

the thrum of ironing sticks
I've not heard
since my mother passed.

SPRING

even April exhausted, all agleam
 with its nightly rain—
my mother, knuckles bit and bloodied,
 salved with wormwood—
why only azaleas blazing
 on her grave?

flowers blown and faded till
 the whole mountainside's bruised
and over the pass to Shooting Star shrine
 a cuckoo's cry
rises up, fresh,
 like a wound in the heart

MUSAN'S TEN BULLS

1. *Searching for the Bull*

Who stamped these left and right prints on my brow?
And who made my self go looking
For my whereabouts, unfindable even for ten million cash?

An arrow that a thousand eyes cannot see,
Which hands cannot grasp, though they extend to knee;
That thief—he steals an abattoir ax, and like an arrow—he's flown.

2. *Finding the Footprints*

O famed physician, a thief's mind's unknowable, even after you
    diagnose his pulse.
Without legal seal, he has sold all the sky and run off
Into lewd joking, into foul words smeared like menstrual blood.

There's evidence he's lived his life treading water,
Those traces, dead and bankrupt, guarded by a barren woman,
The fish that tore the net and escaped, caught once again in the net.

FOR NIRVANA

3. *Seeing the Bull*

The shadow stood, with yoke removed, shining in the shade last
    night,
To heal the laceration, the intangible, as first offense?
I am not yet able to repay the debt of being born into this life.

A shortness of breath, palpitations of the heart—someone is
    suffering in a grave pit, above, in the heavens.
It is a procession out of a funeral village with no one shouldering
    the bier.
It is the second plowing of the life of a son of a mother's
    illicit love.

4. Catching the Bull

Clutching the nose ring—no vitality, no snare,
How many ten-thousand-step wanderings to find the rule to keep
    him bound?
Bandit! Even at death, his life crying with thunder from a cloudless
    sky.

The arrowhead's returning—it's failed to pierce its mark.
I tried to copy the color of skin that tingles with electric pain,
But what a fate—being able to die, caught in the hinge between
    heaven and earth.

13

FOR NIRVANA

5. Taming the Bull

The wasteland of the castle courtyard, with no stone or blade of
    grass—
I have cultivated it, as if for punishment, without a plough or spade,
And now, even if Heaven weeps, I know not how to stay away.

The sky makes a seal: the two letters of the ultimate name,
And the sea—unplumbable by any sounding line—
A paddy field needing five bushels of seed rice to be revived.

6. Riding the Bull Home

The rain stopped at the sound of the gong; the water sounded high in
the valley's sky.
I go bearing news, with the full blossom of a laugh,
Wondering how to bury my soul, and by which family ritual, at my
birthplace.

The dead world is not revivable through a life of crime, and word
gets out
Of my running away to pursue a life of thievery, the selling of others'
goods.
The Yang and Yin symbol remains uncarvable, regardless the burin
one wields.

15

FOR NIRVANA

7. *The Bull Transcended*

It's all right to spit if I have 100 *won* for the fine money.
Just to swallow the hook—as is—what catch could there be?
Even my thoughts of how I've lived have absconded somewhere . . .

The swords of this world—I can find their points with eyes closed,
And the mountain of swords in the next—there are only ten million
    blades.
This world or the next—sell it all off, chew cud day by day.

8. *Both Bull & Self Transcended*

Hee he hee hohohoho uheeheehee uhohoho!
Hahaha uhahaha ueee ee huhuhu
Chuckle, chuckle, *uauae uhoohoohooo hooee!*

An incurable psoriasis has spread over the whole of my body,
My eyes, from my last incarnation, speckled with motes in this
    five-times-twelve-year cycle (as they count it by hand),
The vast 3,000 worlds destroyed by a single thought, a single stick.

9. *Reaching the Source*

Lived with a barren woman, brought a butcher into this world,
Incarcerated myself out of self-doubt while I lived high on usury.
Illicit sex for eons, but—*ah!*—I'm still celibate.

A stone lion by the wayside bit my foot,
But again, since there's no champion to rise up, and the world's fallen
    over backwards in shock,
I, myself, sit up and try embracing this life.

10. *Return to Society*

Getting to like the smell of fish, I'm out at market wearing a money
    belt.
Get married, throw away the legal wife—shall I try living with a
    concubine?
Wooden shoes, those wooden shoes—give one away and still I'm rich.

Sold a wife for 300 *won*,
Plucked out both eyes and sold those for 300 *won*, too.
I am the leper going to beg for food, to the ridge of the barley field
    where the sun comes up—a true leper.

19

FOR NIRVANA

REGARDING MY PENMANSHIP

I looked at the stuff
    I scrawled yesterday:

It's appropriate—like a confession
    of all my life's crimes.

I should've just tossed that brush
    and gone to sleep, right?

The paper, crammed with blood-ink
    I ground from my aching heart,

Spread wide as the sky—is it an affront
    to Heaven?—my body trembles,

Mashed to a pulp, even the source
    of thoughts I wrote just now.

WEEKEND SCRAWL

As he departed last weekend, having rested for the night,
    an old man said,

The world
is like an unraveled thread,
like the skin on a fan,
like the splayed wing of an insect.
His body spread with moxibustion wormwood in the bright blood,
he left,

navel plenty red.

WILD FOXES

One walks into the wordless text,
One walks out,
And when the two meet, each to each,
    they are wild foxes.

HOARSE

Buy into this world, and you're
    saddled with some ingratitude;

The paper's not fit for the floor, but
    still, you stain it with perilla oil;

And—naturally—you've got to let some
    words out beyond those walls.

SPEAKING WITHOUT SPEAKING 1

Eoseongjeon, Gangwon province, on
the funeral day of the potter, Old Man Kim:

There was no funeral ceremony or mourners, but there was a rumor
that his wife, who had died thirty years earlier, appeared with her
hair down, and holding onto his bier, she cried, Look here, look
here! Leave me, leave me, at least your fiery anger when you go! and
the dead Old Man Kim replied, All of my anger, anger, I made into
pottery, pottery.

Actually, this was
a tale told
by the bier-bearers.

SPEAKING WITHOUT SPEAKING 2

an old fisherman from Daepo
on the shore of the East Sea; when he:

goes to the sea—he becomes the sea
goes to the temple—he becomes the temple

wherever his life may go
know him as a wave

SPEAKING WITHOUT SPEAKING 3

don't try to tell me it's good, the valley of the Cave
of the Thousand Buddhas in Outer Seorak

I should be lying there, on that jut of rock
gazing up at the sky

listening to the sound of water
flowing beneath the stone . . .

SPEAKING WITHOUT SPEAKING 4

who painted the mural
in the Museol shrine hall

a stork, a blind carp
in its beak

craning its neck
awaiting the artist's return

SPEAKING WITHOUT SPEAKING 5

On the second of last month
    a head monk came

and asked me the meaning
    of Bodhidharma's coming from the West

I told him that in Inner Seorak's Baekdam Valley
    there are lots of flat rocks.

SPEAKING WITHOUT SPEAKING 6

The rugged farmhand at the temple
working on the dike between the paddies—

Master! Master! People say they hear
the sound of paddy water
flowing through their bodies!

Life is like that—
a paddy with a broken dike,
thirsting endlessly.

WAVES

Reading the sutras deep into the night,
I look up at the dark night sky,

Listen, all alone, to the cry
of the distant sea—

The 1,000 sutras, the 10,000 treatises,
all just waves blown in the wind.

WHAT THE NORTHEAST WIND SAID 1

They're hauling it away,
    they're hauling it away

The ocean's untimely red tide,
    it's bubbling froth,

The mounted bandits of this winter night
    are hauling it all away

FOR NIRVANA

WHAT THE NORTHEAST WIND SAID 2

At an intersection in Seoul's Insadong
    a tall, shadowless tree

Roots in the night sky
    branches in the ground

With a single sprouting leaf
    it covers the whole of the cosmos

WHAT THE SOUTHEAST WIND SAID

Someone is keeping a cocky silence,

and this suffocation, shaking the parched sky, this whole body,

is disrupting the depth of my mid-day nap.

AMDU—DROWNED MAN

Ancient Rules for Everyman 3

Pull him out and pull him out—
  the net is still empty;

In the ocean of *Tripitaka*,
  where countless sentient beings have drowned,

A boatman sits asleep at the prow
  with the sail furled down!

JOJU'S GREAT DEATH

Ancient Rules for Everyman 4

The Buddha—I should have sought him out earlier—
    is nowhere to be seen

The executioner's blade—that life-giving sword—
    falls from an empty sky!

10,000 men have died—
    while one goes on living!

GAESA ENTERING THE BATH

Ancient Rules for Everyman 11

Stop crying, stop crying, stop crying,
    you mourning woman.

Life is the wind outside. And death?
    It is a bend in the river.

This family's news, too—
    that inevitable parting at the end of life.

CHUIMI'S ZEN GONG

Ancient Rules for Everyman 13

Ask, and the askers of the questions
    will all die (if they ask in words).

Far, and again near, in the broken house
    that cast away the sky;

How many tens of thousands of people did you kill,
    sitting there with a single sharp word of the Buddha?

BUDDHA

having let it flow—the water of the waterless river

having let it flood—the water of the waterless river

in the water of the waterless river, a log bridge floats away

CHILDREN OF NAMSAN VALLEY

When the white snow-covered winter passes
The children of Namsan Valley
Go up into the mountain
Where even ten *li* is unimaginably far
And carrying a meadow bunting's egg nest
They return
Having eaten moonlight.

WALKING IN PLACE

villagers toward the sunrise
monks toward the sunset—
life or death, they keep walking

one lifetime
barely as much as a single step
go on, go on
just walking in place

THE PATH OF LOVE

Even love has conditions to meet:
    to love legitimately, one needs

To erect a stone span
    at the neck of the shimmering shallows

And, of course, a trysting place, to
    which this monk and that monk may come

AT THE RAZOR'S EDGE

You bastards who think you're monks,
    consider this: To be a monk

You must die—several times at least—
    at the razor's edge

And the nails of your fingers and toes, your eyebrows,
    all must wither and fall out.

CRIME & PUNISHMENT

That date tree, struck by lightning,
    at the levee by the temple fields

How great was its load of sin—
    it is I who should have been struck

And with thoughts like this, yet again,
    I let the whole day pass

TODAY'S BEAMING

The harvest moon rises, and the clams, with bated breath,
float surfaceward—and open wide their mouths to receive
the moon's beams, revealing all their innermost flesh.

THE WAY TO GYERIMSA TEMPLE

I stagger, single-minded, on the 40-*li*-high path to Gyerimsa,
The black cuckoo of Mt. Chorok soaking in my collar,
Beads of sweat on forehead, white clouds gleaming.

Mountain follows stream and water flows from mountain;
Time means nothing in the landscape of the temple,
One's heart emerges, wordless, exposed—and yet

With these dyed robes weighing heavy on my shoulders
And 108 prayer beads hanging eyeless, tight, around my neck,
Why is the way so dark as I stand in the bright light of day?

In some deep valley, a solitary wildflower blooms with a smile,
And the wind from the great forest comes to drowse in these pine
    woods.
Today, bowing low to the green mountains, at this site, I arrive.

THE WAY FORWARD

Jikjisa Temple Travel Diary 1

water streams down
the path winds upward

I sit with my feet in water
white cloud resting on a slab of stone

my mind in the wide valley
where the cuckoo cries

NOT TWO GATES

Jikjisa Temple Travel Diary 2

over mountain, over waves
barely nightfall—down—both sun and moon

my sole desire, to abide—
even that's all burnt away

the wind leaves a long aftertaste
my heart   opens

SITTING BUDDHA

Jikjisa Temple Travel Diary 3

how heavy is it
the mind seated in its seat?

even if there is no word for why,
lighting the long lamps—sun and moon

watching over each spine of these green hills,
Buddha-head flowers illuminating the dream

BLUE CRANE—ZEN MASTER YEONGHEO

Jikjisa Temple Travel Diary 4

a century of longing behind you,
you left for Yellow Mountain

when you were lonely—the rim of dawn
when you were happy—the moonlit sky

over heaven's vast expanse
do you follow the cosmic law

STONE LAMP

Jikjisa Temple Travel Diary 5

cold stone, warm hand
gather wants, light a lamp

breath burns in the dark
the pine breeze falls asleep

and myself, alone, an owl
crying all night on this vast mountain

COLD LAMP—MASTER WHITE WATER

Jikjisa Temple Travel Diary 6

the Yellow Mountains stretch out
immersed in the distance beyond the sky

winds through the scattered reeds
empty wild field in Geumneung

moon rising, 90,000 *li* night
a cold lamp, burning

MIND MOON

Jikjisa Temple Travel Diary 7

storey after storey, the highest peaks
above the lighted lotus lamps

standing once again on tiptoe
the mind moon rises deep into the heart

even the darkness makes way
as I walk in the center of this night

THE SEAGULLS & THE EAST SEA

Tales from the Temple 2

It happened some time ago. There was an elderly man, not especially holy-looking, but with a certain grace to his old age. He was sitting across from Mt. Nakson, on the very end of the cliff that faces it, a dizzying and precarious place. He was sitting astride a rock all day, looking out at the waves on the surface of the East Sea.

I asked him, "Where are you from, old man?"

He said, "I'm sure I saw two sea gulls flying over the horizon this morning, but they don't seem to be coming back." It sounded like he was talking to himself.

The next day he was at that same spot again, sitting in that same pose, so I asked him, "Did the two sea gulls return?"

He said, "The sea was crying yesterday, but today it's not."

TWO SQUIRRELS

Tales from the Temple 3

This isn't a legend or a story from a once upon a time, it happened just this past year at the hermitage where the nuns come to study. It's deep in the woods, that hermitage. You step into the courtyard, where the foundation stone is buried amongst the trees and the thousand-year-old pagoda is leaning—you can hear the sound of flowing water, and the cry of the black cuckoo permeates your clothes like ink. In the farthest corner of that courtyard there was a stone Buddha, and the devoted women who came to bear sons for the Dharma used to scrape and eat its nose—half of it was eaten away by them. So when you laughed, it looked like the stone Buddha was crying, and when you were actually crying, then it looked like it was laughing. Well, that desolate hermitage might just as well not have been there, but there was an Abbess who had lived there for twenty years. Late that fall, she was standing by the stone Buddha holding on to the shadow of a branch that was floating downstream in the water. She saw two squirrels with acorns in their mouths busily going in and out of a stone wall. She said to herself, "*Aha!* There must be lots of acorns in that wall. We can make an offering of acorn jelly to the Buddha and then eat some ourselves. *Namu Amita Buddha.*" When she knocked down the stone wall, a good bushel of acorns did, indeed, come out of there. But after she got that bushel, she took every last one of the remaining acorns, made jelly, and ate it. The next morning she saw those two poor squirrels chewing on her white rubber shoes. They say those squirrels died eating those white rubber shoes.

THE CRY OF WILD DUCKS

Tales from the Temple 16

Master Mazu and his disciple Paichang were silently walking along a river bank at sunset when they saw a formation of wild ducks flying into the west where the evening sky was dyed red. Suddenly Mazu asked his disciple, "What is that noise?"

"It's the cry of the wild ducks," said Paichang.

They walked in silence for a while, and the Mazu asked again, "Where has the cry of the wild ducks gone?"

"It has gone far off into the west," Paichang replied. But as soon as the words left his mouth, Mazu grabbed Paichang's nose and viciously twisted it.

Paichang screamed "*Ouch! Ouch!*" at the unexpected assault, whereupon Mazu roared like a thunderbolt, "You said it's flown away, but isn't it still here?"

Some time ago, after hearing this story, I asked Abbot Kyoeng-bong of Tongdo Temple, "The flock of wild ducks had obviously flown away. Why did the teacher yell 'isn't it still here'?"

Abbot Kyongbong clicked his tongue and said, "If you were a student, you'd say the cry of the wild ducks is still in the water. Since you're not a student, go have a look at the Buddha floating under the stone bridge. The world you see and hear is inexhaustible, but you'll want to know that the world you can't see or hear is infinite, too . . . *Tsk. Tsk. Tsk.*"

THE OTTER & THE HUNTER

Tales from the Temple 25

A young hunter caught an otter that had come out to the water's edge in search of food and he skinned it and strutted home with its pelt, and the next day he noticed that the otter's bones—which he had thrown away—had left bloody tracks walking off, and so he cautiously followed the trail of blood into a cave, and inside the dark cave he saw the heap of the thin bones that was the mother otter he had skinned and fleshed the day before still alive, and she was embracing her five tiny pups—which had not yet opened their eyes—and they couldn't see their mother's condition, and they were mewling for milk, and the hunter was as cruel as a man could be, but upon seeing the mother and her pups he could not help himself, and so he took the place of the mother otter till the pups were grown; he spent three years like that—which felt to him like three *kalpas*—entirely cutting off the paths of the world and the vagaries of the mind, and the only place someone like him could go after that was to a temple, and the temple refused him because of the gamey odor that exuded from his body, and so he stood in the yard with a brazier of burning charcoal on his head until the crown of his head exploded with a sound like a thunderclap, and only then did the head monk, whose name was Muwoe, heal his wounds with a special mantra, giving him a reason to live and—they say—bestowed upon him the name Hyetong. Of course, all this happened during the reign of King Munmu of Silla.

THE GREEN FROG

Tales from the Temple 29

One morning, after lazily washing my face, I went over to the wall to dump out the water basin. A green frog happened to be sitting in the grass on the other side at that moment and he got a terrible fright—*eek!* He leaped up—all the way up to the top of the wall—and alighted there as if he had slipped. As I saw him lying there panting, flat on his belly, I thought, *This guy is really something, he really is something!* I couldn't get over my admiration for him. But when I tried to compose a sijo poem with that green frog as the subject, I struggled day after day, only to fail in the end. I came to a minor realization: Whatever words I could come up with—for however many *kalpas*—to describe that frog would never do him justice.

THE WAY TO BISEUL MOUNTAIN

Who is that returning on the winding road to Mt. Biseul,
past the trees all stripped of time, the cloud-covered gorges below?

Is it a pheasant that splits the sky with its fluttering wings?
No *keomungo* strings, but if you tread there, won't you hear the rhyme?

The road is spliced—as if to break—cut precipices—extending:
is that scent the spice of hail grains soaked into your clothes?

Does the temple sit, eyes shut, cloaked again in the inky dark?
Just as well to be tucked away, in isolation, obscure.

That lone bird, about now, does it drop a feather as it goes?

2007—SEOUL AT NOON

Today, a nude photo, halfway torn
At a crossroad on an alley wall amid the eateries of Sinsadong

And still, the Earth spins—
Galileo's whine

2007—SEOUL AT NIGHT

Mute tree, mute bird
A picture of me, sitting

Or
An island frozen over in the dark

Not that, either, but a loud bird sneezing

WILD DUCKS & SHADOW

When I ask him—Master Haejang,
hero of the hangover drink—
for tidings of the mountain temple,
he says, Yesterday the wild ducks
that played in the West Star lotus pond
went away, and now, today, only
the shadow of the dogwood remains.

WINTER MOUNTAIN BEASTS

Ate midwinter black bean gruel,
    cast out all manner of demons

Fell asleep reading Master Joju's sayings

Crunch—a frozen tree breaking
    in the deep lonely of a far mountain

A DAY AT OLD FRAGRANCE HALL

The sun slants in, onto the two-tiered wood floor
    of Old Fragrance Hall
Through the hanging plaited bamboo shades,
The whole day flickering away.

Paintings hanging askew on the wall:
    a Taoist hermit with magical powers,
An old ferryman who's let go of the oar,
    drifting with his fishing boat,
And again, so soon, I am the setting sun.

BODHIDHARMA 1

The whole of the West was yours—
and you gave it not a glance

The master, who sat so long in solitude,
purifying himself in flame

Has left us a commodity
at the close of the global exchange

BODHIDHARMA 2

Live—try living—and not
a lucky dream in the world

Even your hereditary occupation
and mooching all used up

Attained your aim for a round, and still
no investors to do business with

BODHIDHARMA 3

A shaman's New Year's offering bowl
left out beneath a boulder—

You ate it all up at a glance,
and even if you were to vomit up the world

Still, you would see no one
Look around—you'll be morning sick

BODHIDHARMA 4

The unfamiliar sound of the wind
that sawed at this one life

With the news cut off
in that apparent space

A pilgrim asks the way
and you draw him an empty circle

BODHIDHARMA 5

Fondle it daily and still
the beard won't grow

The sky, too pale,
is being dyed

Fingernails, toenails, caught in moonlight,
all withered and fallen out

BODHIDHARMA 6

At the notice from afar, of debt returned
at the very conclusion of keeping house

Though this single garment of life
weighs heavy on your shoulders

You block the ways of the world and run—
away—in the opposite direction

BODHIDHARMA 7

On that soft, first-fired clay
on the firm, fertile soil

That bamboo stamped in ink
is a sala tree

On that clear, calm current
you ride upstream

BODHIDHARMA 8

Wash your hair—wash it—
the dandruff doesn't clear

Life is itchy—
you scratch it with your nails

And dark marks,
the scars you left behind

BODHIDHARMA 9

No matter how much you glare,
those sword-blade eyes will not open

That bright seed, crammed in back
and the world not even visible

Declaring the world is all but dead, you chant sutras
in a mourning house to ward off evil spirits

BODHIDHARMA 10

You made the earth quake
with no wind, nor cloud of dust

Thought a firestorm, made Heaven
and Earth echo with your shout

Yet, in the end, you're silent—a dog in a house
of mourning, a dog in a house of mourning

SUNSET, BAY OF INCHEON

That evening the water appeared unusually
    red, red
And the old fisherman, who stayed afloat
    come sweet, come bitter waves
On the next day, was seen
    no longer

THE SEA

Clouds blaze open like peonies
    before the bright sun

Waves, time passing, undulate
    in the thunderous wind and rain

And my heart swells
    a wild goose spreads its wings

WORDS OF A BOATMAN

Against the sky, his palm, fingers all mangled,

Shades his face—no ears, neck, mouth, or nose—

Gathering in the spills of his smile.

MOMENTS I WISHED WOULD LINGER

Mountain echoing to mountain,
    or sea crying out to sea;

Loved ones crossing the water,
    sail raised to catch the wind;

That carefree bum, sitting,
    drowsing in the mountains.

YOU AND I: OUR OUTCRY

At my youthful footsteps,
    or at my polite cough
The mountain stream where the dace
    would leap out of the water
Where did it all flow away to?
    a single crab like a burnt ember

YOU AND I: OUR LAMENTATION

The stone Buddha on the roadside
      where the road splits to my birthplace
and even the holy tree
      hung with 50,000 strips of cloth
Did they ascend to some heaven?
      Mama! Poppa!

SIBLINGS

young siblings ambling down
    the narrow path to the village

like the pink flowers blooming there,
    the color of where stem meets leaf

in the early morning,
    still wet with dew

WHEN THE DAWN COMES DOWN

Here, a grandfather's love is as familiar
    as the taste of bitter orange

And a grandmother's love
    has all the spice of hot pepper paste

I come for a visit, and on the path today
    I taste the morning stillness

A FISTFUL OF ASHES

Day before yesterday, at Mt. Yeongchuk crematorium,
I scattered my longtime dharma friend—a handful of ashes.
The sobs and sniffles of some crying man—I let fly.

The stone marker lying by the road—was it tossed?
It has some breath yet—see the liver spots blooming?
I watched for a long while, then came back down.

After I'm gone—whenever—what will remain?
A blind cuckoo, at least, crying in some forest?
I turn carefully, look back—only a fistful of ashes I've strewn.

HOLDING ON TO A FINGER

there's Master Josil in front of the sangha
    beating the dharma drum

and a kid, maybe 7 years old
    listening, ears plugged

wants to hold my hand
    and hear the sound of thunder

WHEN THE THUNDER GOD
CAME TO MY BODY

Today, out of a mad sky, the thunder god came into my body
saying, Let's smash the world to bits and ride the lightning to the
    West.
Even just a flashing bolt leaves me all choked up.

Peel off this coagulated blood porridge, you'll see
the landmines on the path, not an inch of dirt to bury them,
and thoughts of moving up are a walk, footsteps on that bridge.

Sorrows—they pile up day by day like fallen leaves,
unweighable till the end, the load of freedom.
Long time from now, I'll be alone, unable, to label, this day.

OPENING THE MOUNTAIN-SIDE WINDOW

When I spread out the *Flower Garland Sutra* and open the north
    window,
All manner of birds, names unknown to me, have already
    read it.
Here and there, between the tree branches, they fly . . .

Blades of grass amidst the grasses, lawn bugs amongst the insects,
Trees, shrubs, wild beasts of the mountain, large and small,
Heaven, Earth—all of this—all these lives . . .

Merging into one; and becoming one
They leave their bodies and appear, visible,
Sustenance, each to each, radiant, each other for the one . . .

PROXIMATION

spring coming, and a frog—
that one frog—its incessant croaking

calls me out from sitting
in my cell, and then—

mountain and meadow,
the frozen flora,
ice up and go green again

SUN & MOON

the sky—that high,
the sea—this deep,

the last rays of twilight sunk on the horizon,
clouds like dyed flowers

and the gate of Heaven, opening, as if to close—
Ah!—the moon is rising in the east again

ARISING, PASSING, ATTACHMENT

for Yi Yun-yeong, wife of Son Hak-kyu

In your garden, where autumn passed like a cloudburst,

A single fruit, all the world's flavors clutched inside,

Falls with a *thud*—

A shriveled quince.

THE WIND THAT ONCE WEPT
IN THE PINE GROVE

The wind that once wept in the pine grove
fell asleep—because it was a pine grove

and the wind that once rushed through the great forest
breathed softly—because it was the great forest

that moon, too, passing through the empty sky,
is honest—it cannot be anything but bright

GWANSEUM

The candle-lit dream is melting, dyed with lotus blossom,
Yet after your final bath, you still cannot take the lotus seat.
You are the Bodhisattva who cannot bear the sounds of sorrow.

The 108 prayers in your grasp, the more you count, the heavier
They grow, scattered thoughts strung, bead by bead
As you stand in the moonlit garden, watching over Paradise.

THIS BODY OF MINE

I went up to the top of Namsan and watched the sun go down

Seoul was a dark, red, frothing swamp

And in it, this body of mine, a leech stuck to a duckweed leaf

THE DAY I TRY DYING

The day I get the death notice
    I try dying myself—

Build a coffin, close my eyes,
    lie down inside;

Sprinkle blue-smoke ashes
    from the oven of the crematorium.

AS I LOOK UPON MYSELF

Sitting, in the meditation hall,
I look upon myself—

a single bug crawling by
stretches its body, contracts it;

gnawing at all manner of things,
it evacuates, but

also does lay its eggs.

WANING LANDSCAPE

Are they weeping, or laughing, as they go
The geese from the reed forest flying in a flock
And the sky, the autumn sky, its throat sunk in the kill

AT THE TOMB OF KING SEONDEOK

Late fall flowers, blooming in the cold wind,
look up to the pale daylight moon.

Your throne didn't last a hundred years,
but the dirt you return to abides a thousand.

In the empty mountain where the scops owl cries,
only a rain of pine needles piling up.

FOREST

To live like that,
to go on living like that

Mountains forming valleys
to let the waters flow

And trees breeding insects
under their rough bark

NEW SHOOTS

The sky, the eye's light,
    open once more at the point of breath,

An ember born again
    where a star's light glanced—

Today, at last, the green waves
    of May come surging again.

EARLY SPRING

A plantain leaf, half the spring day
at my western window,

its image like calligraphy ink
bleeding into cheap draft paper—

raindrops fall into the blaze
of sunbeams in the valley of roof tiles.

THREE VIEWS OF SPRING

1. *The Spring Purge*

the fiery rashes in my crotch
have caused my festering molars, all, to fall out—
my ignorance, wide as the sky, *ah*, that magical purge

2. *A History of Spring*

I cut my words with my tongue—a blade for beheading horses,
and even hallucinogenic mushrooms, which claimed my soul,
are all budding like flowers on this damned spring night

3. *Spring Riot*

thirsty—thirsty—even the nectar in the blossoms
each passing spring withers my ever-diminishing life,
and this year it appears the flowers will come in one big riot

THE SOUND OF MY OWN CRY

In the woods at noon
I hear a bird cry out

On the shore, mid-morning,
I hear the gulls

When will I hear
The sound of my own cry?

ALL THE SAME AT JOURNEY'S END

age: twelve
identity: monk

work till noon stomping the foot mill,
split firewood till the sun goes down

once a generation, hear the cry
of a bird hiding out in the woods

then ten years, twenty years,
forty years pass, and today

living on the mountain
not seeing the mountain

and the sound of the bird's cry?
i can't even hear my own

SCARECROW

He waves at the flocking birds,
At the man walking by—
This scarecrow, as he works for others, with a smile

A year of bounty, or a famine year,
Take a walk along the paddy dikes—
Mine, yours—
See the field, the autumn wind?
Not a sole possession, yet I, too, a smiling scarecrow

Is what they say I am,
But clear my mind, spread my two arms wide, and
Everything, even the sky—all just a single step away

DAYS LIVING ON THE MOUNTAIN

Reached the age when I'm sick of it all.
My thoughts, too, knotty like the bones of my bent back,
Today I grabbed a stump about to fall over.

Day before yesterday, I went to see Master Hancheon at his temple
And asked him what made him want to go on living.
He couldn't explain in words, so he told me to strike the
  cloud gong.

Now, really, the days living on the mountain—
One day crying like a bug in the grass,
One day laughing like a flower in the field,
Only to see it—the flow that ends the flow.

VAPORS

No way forward, no way back
Look around—in all directions, up and down—
    empty sky and endless cliff

Funny
What I wandered all my life to find is a precipice
Finally at this cliff, where I must
    toss down both life and death—
Vapors waft around to their hearts' content
Funny
That what I clung to all my life—nothing but vapors

MY LIFELINES

what I've been seeking all my life
are the mainlines, the veins
of Zen
& poetry

the conclusion I reached today—
poetry is woodgrain, knotted,
& Zen is wood's grain, straight

EMBERS (AFTERWORD)

—to my readers

These words I've spewed 'til now—they're all drivel.
Mouth ajar at last, as not to tread on earth or stone,
This body, infused with brass, in a molten fire.

ON TRANSLATING THE UNTRANSLATABLE
Musan Cho Oh-hyun's Poems as *Hwadu* Practice

Heinz Insu Fenkl

METHOD

MY INITIAL TRANSLATIONS of Master Cho's poems were done in the "traditional" way, that is, with an eye toward both lexical correspondence and equivalency of meaning in the target language, which happens to be English in this case. Several of the poems in this volume (e.g., "As I Look Upon Myself") follow this method and also represent how I applied the syllabic constraints of the sijo form to English in order to parallel the original structures.[1]

But I soon found that a traditional rendition in the target language could not do the poems justice. The approach I had to take was more like Zen archery. The issue wasn't just the linguistic complexity of the original poems, it was that even underlying all the layers of wordplay and superposition of imagery, Master Cho's poems were fundamentally a part of his practice—they were *Zen* poems. To try understanding them in Korean required an approach parallel to the tackling of a Zen koan. A Korean koan (*gongan*) is generally built on a *hwadu* (話 頭)—a "word head," that is to say a point on which the koan spins—or, I think more accurately, a seed crystal upon which the meaning of the koan crystalizes and blooms. A koan is notoriously difficult—it is not a test of one's rational intelligence (despite the many commentaries, cribs, and solution books one can find these days). A koan engages the full being, and its comprehension is reflected in the full being of the student—what appears as the verbal solution is merely an epiphenomenon.

Master Cho's poems have a similar quality. Their surface is easy to read and comprehend—very smooth in the source language. Their narrative quality, their allusions, and their use of understood tropes allow one to arrive at an "apparent" poem without requiring deep reflection. They can be appreciated aesthetically on this first pass. But the first pass only reveals a single layer or facet of the poem, which then leaves a kind of resonance—an image, a word, a phrase will linger naggingly in memory, like an echo. This brings one back to the poem to read again and to discover another narrative, theme, or poem in superposition. Then the process happens again. Each layer of this process would produce a different translation because the associative layering of words and images works differently in Korean and English.

One could say the above about poetry in general, but it is amplified to a remarkable degree in Master Cho's work. One must remember that Zen poetry is inherently ironic, as the basic tenet of Zen is antithetical to text. Zen is the direct transmission of the Buddhist teaching *without reliance on words or symbols*. But Zen practice also understands the ironic necessity of language as a means of communication—it is, after all, the finger that points at the moon. One does not want to focus on the finger, but it is a useful pointing device. In Mahayana Buddhism, of which Zen is a part, one common analogy is that the teachings of the Buddha—including texts based on his sermons—are like the boat that one rides to the other shore. Once across, one does not need to—or want to—carry the boat around any longer. It becomes an unwanted burden.

So I have approached Master Cho's poems as a kind of *hwadu* practice. I have read them and reread them many times, but I have willfully made it a point not to memorize them either in the original Korean or in the translation. I have looked up many words—as translators are wont to do—but I did not memorize the etymologies or the definitions, and thus I have often looked up the same word numerous times in both Korean and in corresponding Chinese characters, as if I were seeing it again for the first time. This allowed for the discovery of new associations in new contexts, something that would have been unlikely to happen if I had simply memorized corresponding words and taken for granted that I knew and understood them.

I consider all of these translations both provisional and ephemeral. When I look at my translations now, I am reminded that in Buddhism the self is an illusion. These poems were translated by another self—an earlier ego self of an earlier time. I can often see into the workings of that earlier consciousness engaging with the emergent consciousness that wrote the initial poem in Korean, and the confluence of those various minds[2]—their interpenetration (*tongdal* in Korean)—is what Master Cho's poems illustrate for me. Multiple facets of the poem, in both original and translation, emerge and interpenetrate, thereby demonstrating the interrelation of minds.

THE BACKSTORY

These translations came about in a rather unexpected way. I had not known about Master Cho's poetry until I was invited to participate in Harvard University's fifth-annual Sijo Festival, held in the spring of 2010. I had arrived late the first night just after all the events had concluded. Luckily, I was able to obtain a program package before I checked into the hotel for the evening. It was around midnight when I finally went to bed after browsing through the enclosed booklet, which included five translations of Cho Oh-hyun's poems by David McCann and seven others in their original Korean.

Master Cho's poems struck me as especially challenging. He was lucky to have someone of David McCann's abilities offering his work in English. McCann, a gifted poet in his own right (and having translated major Korean poets like Kim Chi-ha, So Chongju, and Ko Un), was able to convey far more than the surface of the sijo he had chosen to translate. But when I looked at the original texts I saw that they were, almost by definition, *impossible* to translate. They had the sensibility of casual koans, the same confounding of language. Coming from a Zen tradition, that was to be expected, yet it was not the kind of challenge a translator would typically have to face. I knew Master Cho was scheduled to be at the conference and was expecting to meet him at breakfast the next morning, where I was looking forward to talking with him and David McCann about the challenge of translating his work. After quickly reading through the booklet and the program, I went to sleep.

A couple of hours later I bolted upright in bed, awakened so suddenly from a dream that I didn't initially recognize where I was. I was entirely disoriented until I noticed the red LED alarm clock, which read 3:33. The dream had been especially vivid and semi-lucid, so I remembered it as if it were waking life.

I had been walking in the mountains. From the trail I was on I could look across a valley and see a range of snowcapped peaks in the distance stretching across the horizon. I had been traveling for some time and was tired—I could feel the sweat on my body and even the cool breeze of that high elevation. The air was especially crisp but also oddly dense as it often is in dreams. It had a palpable quality to it, the kind of viscosity one feels in the air while doing qigong. I was aware that I was in a dream, and I knew I was a monk. I was wearing black robes and carrying a simple staff. I approached the mountaintop inn, which had the typical wine-seller's banner flapping out front, and I went inside. The place was empty except for one customer. He was sitting on an elevated floor at a low table, also wearing black robes, which I recognized as those of my own order. But he was wearing a straw rain hat and I couldn't see his features. As I stood over him he tilted his head back until I could see his face. He was a relatively young monk, perhaps in his late thirties, but I instantly recognized him as Cho Oh-hyun. I greeted him and introduced myself. He had been expecting me, he said. He asked me to join him at his table, but as I began to unsling my sack, he looked up at me and said, very clearly: "You—it's time to receive the language of Korean Buddhism." As he spoke those ten words in Korean, he raised his right hand and pointed at my chest with his first two fingers. A sudden bolt of energy leapt from his fingers into my solar plexus. It was like a tremendous electrical shock, and that is what made me bolt upright in bed and wake up.[3]

I was sweating. I had slept with the window open a crack, so there was a cool breeze coming into the hotel room. As I recalled the dream, the first thing I wondered was why Cho Oh-hyun was so young. I had heard he was in his early eighties. And why was he wearing black robes and not gray Korean robes? It made sense to me that my dream self was wearing black robes because I was wearing a black Tibetan jacket, but I would have expected a Korean monk to be wearing gray.

My body was still full of that strange energy, and I knew I could not get back to sleep. Even if this was simply a message from my unconscious, I took it to mean that I should try translating the remaining poems in the program booklet before meeting master Cho at breakfast.

So I stayed up and translated three of Master Cho's sijo before snatching an hour of sleep and learning, when I got up again, that he had not come. That was the time of the H1N1 pandemic, and he had been concerned about the possibility of getting sick on the airplane. He had sent a proxy instead. I read my translations at the festival, where I was also privileged to meet Professor Kwon Youngmin and the sijo poet Hong Sung-ran for the first time.

Later, after the Harvard Sijo Festival, while I was doing research for my new translation of *Kuunmong*, the seventeenth-century Korean Buddhist classic by Kim Man-jung, I was looking into the history of Chinese Buddhism and I learned that some Chan monks wore black robes.[4] The mountains in my dream were like the Seoraksan range in Korea, but they were also much taller, as if they were simultaneously Seoraksan, the mythic Five Sacred Mountains of China, and the Four Sacred Mountains of Buddhism. If the monk I'd met in the dream was of the same order, we were perhaps part of a lineage that went back to a Tang Dynasty Chinese Chan order. What the monk had said to me was very specific and full of multilayered wordplay in keeping with the nature of Master Cho's poetry. In Korean, it was "*Janae han bul mal talttaega dwesso.*" Every word had multiple meanings, and even today, five years later, those layers of meaning continue to shift for me.[5] My initial understanding was that he was telling me it was time to learn the language of Korean Buddhism—figuratively, it was time for me to "ride the horse" or "receive the word" (i.e., *mal tada*) of "Korean Buddhism" (i.e., *han bul*).

Master Cho is of the Gusan or "Nine Mountain" Zen lineage,[6] which traces back to the great Tang Dynasty monk Huineng (638–713, the sixth and last Patriarch of Chan Buddhism), through Nanyue Huairang (677–744), Mazu Daoyi (709–788), and three others.[7] Mazu Daoyi was of particular interest to me because in Korean his name is Majo Doil (馬祖道一). He was known for his "strange words and extraordinary actions," just like Master Cho. The readings of the Chinese characters was quite a shock to me:

馬 = *ma* = horse   祖 = *jo* = grandfather/ancestor
道 = *do* = Tao   一 = *il* = one.

The *cho* (曺 *jo*) in Master Cho's name Cho Oh-hyun (曺五鉉) is a surname character (interior of a room, or a room), but in Korean it sounds the same as the character for "grandfather" or "forefather." The *oh* (五) in his name is the Chinese character for the number five, which is homophonous for the sign of the horse[8] and also for "awakening."

My dream almost seems to have been an exegesis of Master Cho's name from a time before I had investigated its underlying associations. He signs his poetry 雪嶽霧山 (Seorak Musan), or "Musan of Seorak," whose Chinese characters are snow/peak/fog/mountain. In keeping with the multilayered nature of his poetry, the name Musan written in alternate Chinese characters—霧散—can be read as "to dissipate like mist." The fog on the mountain is not obstructive—it clears itself. Another homophonous reading of Musan—無山—makes the mountain itself disappear; it means "No Mountain"!

Two other readings of the *mu* in Master Cho's Buddhist name were hidden among the secondary and tertiary homophonic readings of the Chinese character, but they were also related to my dream. There is a *mu* that means "to be on fire," or "fire": 燶 (*bultal mu* or *bul mu* in Korean); and another *mu*, which includes the horse radical in it, meaning to run swiftly: 驚 (*dallil mu*).

EXEGESIS: WHOLE MOON AND PENETRATING MOON

After my surprise at not seeing Master Cho at breakfast the next day,[9] I understood my dream meeting with him to be one of those fateful and ironic synchronicities. The blast of energy in my solar plexus had done its job, and the need to translate his poetry stayed with me so profoundly that I applied it as a form of meditative practice. I read his poems in Korean and then reflected on them while doing Vipassana meditation so that I could retrace their associative trajectories through the *skandhas*.[10] I monitored my bodily sensations along with the associative connections, in keeping with the body-scanning process of Vipassana and the feeling of the energy body in qigong. I tried to maintain those networks of associations and sensations as I re-created the poems in English. The process was not so much that of translating a word or element but the "deep structure"—the relationship among the elements in the poem, then the relationship between the words and the reader, and then the relationships among the relationships evoked by the words in both contexts.

In some ways I was not entirely sure of my translation method, born of a dream meeting with Master Cho and applying the kinesthetic "reading" of my reading process via Vipassana. But in my research, I learned that the great Tang Dynasty monk Yongjia Xuanjue (665–713), known in Korea as Yongga Hyeongak, had said:

Neither try to eliminate delusion nor search for what is real. This is because ignorance, just as it is, is the Buddha Nature. This worldly body itself, which appears and disappears like a phantom, is nothing other than the reality of life. When you actually wake up to the reality of life, there is not any particular thing to which you can point and say, "This is it."[11]

I found validation in Hyeongak's words. Likewise, I could see that Master Cho had resolved his own deep engagement with the incompatibility of Zen and language by applying and transcending binary distinctions, which often collapse into something absolutely commonplace in his poems. I was reminded of the one called "My Lifelines":

what I've been seeking all my life
are the mainlines, the veins
of Zen
& poetry

the conclusion I reached today—
poetry is woodgrain, knotted,
& Zen is wood's grain, straight[12]

The imagery of this poem left me in between the straight and the knotted, thinking of wavy woodgrain, or grain like water, and it took me to the image of waves swirling into a circular knot and unwinding again. It took me also to one of Master Cho's prose pieces, which he later chose as the preface for this book.

The epigraph that begins the preface—*The moon in the water*—is Master Cho's allusion to *The Song of Enlightenment* by Yongga Hyeongak.[13] To provide a context for the epigraph, let me quote a few additional lines:

鏡裏看形見不難
It is not hard to see forms in a mirror,
水中捉月爭拈得
But the moon in the water—who can grasp it?

*   *   *

一月普現一切水
One moon is reflected in all waters—

一切水月一月攝

All moons in all waters are that one moon.

Master Cho's preface is one of his story sijo (as discussed by Professor Kwon Youngmin in the introduction), and its use of the allusion to the moon on the water is a poetic illustration of two of the most important principles in Korean Buddhism: *muae* and *tongdal*. *Muae* (無礙) is generally translated as "non-obstruction," and *tongdal* (通達) is usually translated as "interpenetration."[14] Written in *hangul*, without the Chinese characters, *tongdal* sounds like "whole moon." The water reflects but does not obstruct (i.e., *muae*) the whole moon (i.e., *tongdal*). At the same time, the Gwaneum Pond is both an illustration of and a play on the concept of *tongdal* as well—it is a *tong* (container) for the *dal* (moon), in other words, a *daltong* for *tongdal*.

A man trying to grasp the moon in the water penetrates it. He is likewise penetrated by the moon's light, which itself is an illusion, since it is the sun's light reflected. He cannot grasp the moon, but the man can realize its light has penetrated him. There is also some poetic humor here, a lighthearted warning about trying too hard to grasp the moon. The great Tang poet Li Po drowned trying to embrace the moon in the water. Fortunately, in Master Cho's story sijo, the man leaves through the temple gate after his realization just as dawn is breaking. The sun—the source of the light reflected by the moon—is coming up. This story sijo is the perfect preface for Musan's Zen sijo, which, just like the ungraspable moon in the water, point you at the original source of light.

I hope my translations have helped his poems do the same for you.

This essay, in an earlier and shorter form, was presented as a keynote address at the Korea on the Global Stage Symposium, Sound of Human Spirit: Musan Cho Oh-hyun, held at the David Brower Center at the University of California, Berkeley, March 20, 2015, sponsored by the Center for Korean Studies and the Institute of East Asian Studies.

1. Applying syllabic parallelism in English to Japanese haiku tends not to work well, but the more open and flexible structure of Korean sijo makes this possible.

2. One often refers to a point of view or consciousness as being in a literary work, but it is important to remember that that is just a figure of speech we should not take for granted. What we attribute to the work is actually our minds triggered by the symbols in the text, which plays our consciousness like a musical score.

3. When I finally met Master Cho at the symposium in his honor at UC Berkeley, one of the things he mentioned was that the great Tang poet Tu Fu said he wrote poetry to shock the reader.

4. In 2011, about a year after the Harvard conference, I also saw Banmei Takahashi's *Zen*, a film on the life of Dōgen Zenji, in which Dōgen meets black-robed Chan monks in China in the thirteenth century.

5. Every word could mean something else, beginning with *janae*, which is just "you" on the surface but could be a reference to the fact that I was sleeping.

6. The current name, Jogye, was adopted in 826.

7. Bodhidharma (470–543) was the first Patriarch of Zen. His successors were Huike (487–593), Sengcan (d. 606), Diaoxin (580–651), Hongren (601–674), and finally Huineng (638–713).

8. *junma* (준마—駿馬: 빠르게 잘 달리는 말) as in "a horse that runs swiftly and well." Horse symbolism seems to be important to me. My first essay

in *Azalea: Journal of Korean Literature & Culture* 1 (2007), published by the Harvard University Korea Institute, included an explication of the Korean Heavenly Horse and its connection to dream, language, and light in Lee Chang-dong's first short story, "The Dreaming Beast" (pp. 338–56).

9. I did not actually meet Master Cho in person (or communicate with him directly) until the morning of the Berkeley symposium nearly five years later, on March 20, 2015.

10. In Buddhism, these are *form, sensation, perception, mental formations,* and *consciousness*—the five "heaps" or "aggregates" that constitute our understanding and perception of mundane reality. The *skandhas* also constitute our very sense of identity. In Zen, all things constituted of *skandhas* are inherently empty of independent existence.

11. As quoted by Kosho Uchiyama (1912–1998), Zen abbot of Antai-ji, in giving instructions on zazen practice.

12. The concept of *che-yong* (體用), or "essence function," also central to Korean Buddhism, is often illustrated via the metaphor of a tree. It is a way of cutting through the binary distinction of absolute and conditional reality.

13. 永嘉證道歌, known as *Jeungdoga* in Korean.

14. These principles were central to the teaching of the great Silla-period monk Weonhyo (617–686) and the Hwaeom (Flower Garland) School of Korean Buddhism.

ACKNOWLEDGMENTS

MANY THANKS TO the Manhae Foundation and Professor Kwon Youngmin for their generosity and support. Thanks also to Professors David McCann and Lee Young-Jun for introducing me to the work of Musan Cho Oh-hyun at the 2010 Sijo Festival sponsored by Harvard University's Korea Institute. Special thanks to our intern, Bella Dalton-Fenkl, and to David Lee and Peter Camilleri.